# Soul Wisdom

All net profits from the sale of this book
*Soul Wisdom: A Guide To Miraculous Living, Book 1*
are being donated to charities benefiting children.

To order additional copies:

Visit:

www.lauriesmith.com

Or send your request to:

Spreading Sunshine Books
P.O. Box 692
Tiburon, CA 94920

# Soul Wisdom

## A Guide to Miraculous Living, Book 1

Laurie E. Smith

Spreading Sunshine Books
San Francisco, CA

Copyright © 2000, 2007 by Laurie E. Smith, All rights reserved.
Library of Congress Cataloging Card Preassigned Number has been applied for.
ISBN: 978-0-9778022-0-3

First printing: April 2007

Printed in the United States of America.
This book may not be reproduced in whole or in any part or any form whatsoever including the scanning, uploading or distribution via the Internet; in the form of a phonographic recording or photographic copy; or by any other means for private or public use other than for "fair use" as brief quotations embodied in articles and reviews without the prior written permission of the copyright owner and publisher. The author intends this book to only offer information. In the event that you choose to use this information for yourself and your own life, the author and publisher take no responsibility for your actions. The author and publisher are in no way liable for any misuse of the material.

To Jim,

Thank you for seeing me through yet another dream-come-true.
The first, of course, was you.

To Devin James,

May you always know what a bright Light you are.
Thank you for shining into our lives.

# Invitation

If you have picked up this book, chances are, perhaps for reasons still unknown to you, your paths are meant to cross. Yes, I do mean your path and the path of this book. You see, in many ways, this book has a life of its own.

When people ask about how I wrote the words on these pages, I pause. That's because I don't view the words in this book as written by me. Instead, they happened to me.

That's why I'm asking you a favor. I'm asking you to be open. I have no idea what unique gifts are in store for you as you embark on this adventure. All I know is *Soul Wisdom* has a powerful energy, an energy that has changed my life forever.

I am sharing this book to extend my immense gratitude to Spirit, as well as my absolute confidence that you have an incredible and unique ability to receive amazing insights and direction for your own life.

May you trust your wisdom within, and have your own personal awakening as you travel these pages. I wish you and *Soul Wisdom* a magnificent journey together. I wish you miracles.

# Contents

Awakening To Miracles ... i

1. Miracles ... 1

2. Love ... 7

3. Health ... 15

4. Spirit ... 21

5. Shadow ... 27

6. Spiritual Sight ... 35

7. Self Love ... 41

8. Mission ... 47

9. Present Moment ... 49

10. Words To Live By ... 53

Acknowledgements ... 70

# Awakening to Miracles

*"These are the voices which we hear in solitude, but they grow faint and inaudible as we enter into the world"*

-Ralph Waldo Emerson, *Self-Reliance*

On the day this book began to be written, I was struggling. I was having trouble pin-pointing what was wrong, exactly. No matter what I did, however, I couldn't shake the feeling that something wasn't quite right. I now realize that was probably the first sign my soul wisdom—the voice of my inner, truest self—was trying to get my attention.

If you had been an acquaintance or even a close friend of mine at this point in my life, you probably wouldn't have noticed anything was wrong. I was running a successful media relations business, married to a wonderful man, and lived in a beautiful home in a nice neighborhood.

Inside, however, part of me knew something was *not right*. I decided to leave my office early, go home and do what I normally did on particularly bad days—call a friend and complain about everything wrong with my life. When I arrived home and walked toward the phone however, a voice in my head directed me to instead sit down and write.

Reluctantly, I sat down before my laptop. As soon as my fingers hit the keyboard, they began to type as if they were separate from my body. By this time in my life, I had studied many different forms of holistic healing and energy work. Intuitive messages had never come to me quite this directly, however, or in quite this way.

Although I was skeptical, I was also feeling desperate. I wanted answers, enough to push through my fear and doubts, and keep listening to the messages I was receiving.

After the first afternoon, I wrote almost every day for several months, recording everything I felt, heard and saw. I felt more like a scribe than a writer. I would simply turn on my laptop, enter a deep state of meditation and type whatever words or experiences I had as they were happening, usually with my eyes closed. Sometimes guides showed up, like characters with specific stories.

Other times, I heard just a single voice. I also had very clear visions, feelings and sensations during the process. It was almost as if I was taking a course, receiving a connected series of lessons from many different teachers.

I didn't reread the messages until they all had been recorded. I simply made a commitment to try to apply the lessons of this unexpected, new program of education to my life in the best way I could. At the end, I was surprised at how well everything flowed together and at some of the things that had been said.

The messages I received have formed the curriculum within two books. This book, *Soul Wisdom*, focuses primarily on the messages that came from one voice, whom I call Wise Spirit. The second book *Spirit In Disguise* includes messages from many different sources whom I call Wise Friends.

As I worked with the material, I found myself struggling with implementing it into my everyday life. To help myself and others with this process, I have developed a program called *Dancing With The Divine: A Nine-Week Adventure in Manifesting Miracles*. More information about this and my other programs can be found on my website at www.lauriesmith.com.

## Accepting Life's Mysteries

Around the same time I was receiving this material, I had many other experiences that caused me to question assumptions I had made about the world. One such experience stands out in particular. It was around the time of New Year's Eve and I had just completed a five-day juice and raw vegetable fast, which I had heard was a great way of making a fresh start.

On the last day of the fast, I meditated, then went outside for a walk during which I met one of our very dear older neighbors, who has since passed away. She was a devout Christian and always seemed filled with a sense of wonder and delight for the world around her.

As this woman was talking, I noticed all around her body an amazingly beautiful, glowing yellowish golden light. Thinking I was seeing things, I kept moving my eyes from her face to her shoulder. No matter what I did, I could not make this light around her disappear.

Knowing nothing about the human energy field at the time, I visited a small holistic bookstore. After perusing the titles on the shelves, I decided to purchase a little book entitled *How To See and Read the Aura* by Ted Andrews. The more I learned, the more passionate I became about the miraculous energy that is all around us. I decided to continue my own exploration by taking workshops and training programs in energy work and other modalities of healing. I was fortunate my media relations business allowed me the flexibility and the financial means to do this.

One of the programs I enrolled in was a Feng Shui certification training program called The Accelerated Path©, led by Nancy SantoPietro, a Feng Shui Expert/Chakracologist, and Author of *Feng Shui & Health:The Anatomy of A Home*. Throughout the program, Nancy would lead us through guided meditations. At one point during a break, she pulled me aside and mentioned she had noticed my head jerking and bobbing back and forth while I was meditating.

I had noticed this too, but had assumed this was something that happened to everyone. Nancy mentioned that I might be channeling. I had never heard the word "channel" used in this way, and asked her what she meant. She said perhaps some higher energy was looking to come through me.

Although I hadn't known it as 'channeling,' I had experienced something that seemed to fit what she described. Earlier in the same day, we had done a meditative exercise with partners. We were supposed to face one of our classmates, close our eyes and try to get some intuitive information about her. When it was my turn to read my partner's energy, I felt very nervous that I wasn't going to receive any useful information.

Then, in my mind's eye, I saw a vision of a Native American woman, with a long black braid down the middle of her back. This female guide offered to do the intuitive reading for me because I was so nervous. I then felt the strangest sensation as she entered my body through the crown of my head.

Because she was much larger in physique than I was, I felt my body expand; it almost felt as if my skin was stretching. I could even feel her braid down my back as I "became" her. I felt incredibly calm and peaceful as this experience happened. I then received many pieces of information about my fellow classmate that were surprisingly accurate, including images of some items in her home, which I had never visited.

While the Native American guide I saw appeared much like a real person, more often, guides appear to me as a silhouette of color, like the glowing outline of a person. I frequently see guides like this while sharing Reiki, a form of energy work typically done while a client is laying down and fully clothed. Sometimes, these guides give me information about how to help a client. Almost always, they are right, far more so than I would have been had I directed the session with my rational mind.

A particularly powerful example of this happened during the internship process of my Reiki training. I was working an acquaintance who had asked me to assist her with some physical challenges. Because she was someone I knew personally, and because I just beginning to work with clients professionally, I had a very strong desire to help her 'heal' — both from my personal desire to help as well as from my insecurities as a new student.

We had a very deep and long session together. After about an hour of working together, four figures outlined by a green, glowing light suddenly appeared, two at the woman's shoulders, the other two at her feet. These four spirits communicated very clearly to me that it was not my job to 'heal' this woman, that I had done enough, and some of what my client was experiencing physically, she needed to heal in her own way, for some positive purpose. As I leaned away from my client's body, I saw these glowing figures step in, bow over her, and put their hands on her to help me finish the Reiki session. Watching this happen, I felt deep humility and gratitude.

This event was a powerful lesson for me in how important it is to honor deep intuitive information, especially when it feels as if it is coming from a positive source, and to constantly be aware of my own 'human stuff.' Ever since that experience, I have set an intention before every Reiki session and meditation I do to be as clear of a channel as possible to whatever is in my and my client's highest purpose, knowing I rarely know what that is.

During this time in my life, I found intuitive insights also began coming more easily to me, especially when my heart was open and my intentions clear. For example, when I was with the client described above, I saw several black dots in the energy above her right breast (she was fully clothed). When I mentioned this to her, she shared with me that, while this was not the specific physical problem she was seeking healing for, she did have cysts in that breast that her physician was monitoring.

I have learned that, when it comes to accessing higher energies or intuitive information, it is not so much about certain things *we* need to do, but rather it is about making space—in other words, getting out of the way—so a higher power can connect with us. When I have remembered that, I have often received information or have had an experience that has helped me or another person in some miraculous way.

## Straddling Two Worlds

As I began to expand the energy healing and spiritual life coaching work I was doing, I still kept my media relations business afloat to help pay the expenses of day-to-day living. Since my media relations specialty was working with pharmaceutical companies, I felt a bit as if I had one foot in one world, rooted heavily in science and 'real world' rules, and one foot in the holistic, spiritual world—whose rules, if there were any, I didn't fully know or understand; it just seemed as if anything was possible. The deeper my holistic, spiritual work became, the further apart the two worlds seemed to grow, with me left dangling in the middle.

For a long time, I felt like I was living a closeted life, hiding what seemed most real to me from the rest of the world. Although I had been exposed to spiritual concepts my entire life as the daughter of a Presbyterian minister, I had never heard anything in church about what I was experiencing. I was hesitant to share my experiences with anyone other than my clients and fellow students, including some of my family members and closest friends.

Fortunately, when I finally did share what had been happening to me with those closest to me, I was overcome by the support I received. I feel incredibly grateful for all the people in my life who have not only accepted me, but who have also entrusted me with their own deeply personal stories of revelation and awakening.

## Trusting Joy

Making the decision to honor the wisdom of one's soul isn't always easy. It can bring into question our very sense of who we are. If we really listen to the truth bubbling up beneath the surface of our lives, things might change. We might have to face the fact that our inner wisdom and that which we have come to accept as true, safe and popular may be very different—a process that can be rather disconcerting, to say the least.

Fortunately, something happens when we listen to the soul. The soul gets ecstatic. It's almost as if, after being ignored for so long, our truest, divine self is delighted to finally be noticed, and will do anything to keep the relationship humming along.

Even when I was resisting, one thing that has kept me moving forward on my soul's path has been the joy I feel while doing this work. There is a section in this book in Chapter Six on *Spiritual Sight* that says:

> *"At certain times in your life, I have given you each a secret, an epiphany...You will remember it as having been a moment of intense and complete joy...Look to that moment. Therein lies your own formula for seeing through the eyes of Spirit. You will know when you are seeing the world as Spirit, because you will recognize that feeling of joy."*

Receiving the information in this book and its companion *Spirit In Disguise* was one of the happiest, most incredible, blissful experiences in my life. I had no idea so much happiness could be experienced by simply sitting in a chair.

When I'm connecting with a higher source through meditation, I am happy. Life flows. Miraculous things happen. On the other hand, when I am blocking, resisting, or any part of me is criticizing the process by which connection happens for me, I feel deep discontent, much like I was feeling on the day when this book started to be written.

As much as I love working with clients and energy, I have found that what feels even more right for me is helping others recognize that they too have the ability to connect, intimately and directly, with something greater. I'll never forget seeing that familiar smile or look of amazement creep across a student's face when she has just connected with a high level of energy or has had some type of experience she never before realized was possible.

# Letting Go

For many years after the material in these books was recorded, I felt very protective, almost the way a mother is with a newborn. To a great extent, the information in this book and *Spirit In Disguise* became the foundation for my work with clients and the meditation and spiritual life coaching workshops I taught. However, I was still hesitant to share the material specifically. These books seemed somehow inextricably connected with my self.

Another reason I resisted was because, for a long time, I thought I needed to fully integrate the information into my own daily way of living before I could share it.

Although it has been a constant focus of my life to live as the words on these pages recommend, some days I do better than others. For a long time, I felt uncomfortable delivering information I was still learning myself.

As years passed after recording this material, I kept battling with Spirit, asking, questioning, challenging. "Am I really supposed to share it?" I felt more comfortable keeping it on the shelf of my office, carefully guarded. Like all creations, however, I have come to understand that the messages I received have their own path to follow, and their own timing in which they needed to be set free.

## How to Use *Soul Wisdom*

This book can be used in several different ways. I invite you to have fun exploring what works for you. I am continually finding new ways to integrate its meaning into my own life. While the material in this book may sound as if it is coming directly from Spirit, I believe God really does speak to each of us in "different tongues." It is my hope that the messages in this book inspire you to connect with your own inner voice and to trust the unique way a higher energy is communicating with you.

This book is not meant to reflect any specific religious perspective. In fact, the overall meaning weaving throughout this work is that we each receive universal spiritual messages in different forms, and that each and every one of us, regardless of religious following or origin of birth, are connected to Spirit and each other.

I invite you to change words or phrases in your personal copy of the book so the terminology feels most right to you. If at any time while reading this book, you feel discomfort, be gentle with yourself and tune inward to see if perhaps a growth opportunity might be at hand. It can also be helpful to remember that sometimes, discomfort means we are being stretched or on the verge of a major turning point or revelation.

Pace yourself as you read the material. Take breaks. Remember to breathe. Go at whatever speed feels most right to you.

You might want to choose a chapter that calls to you by its title—perhaps you are seeking guidance on a specific issue, like dealing with health or relationship issues. Chapter 10, *Words to Live By*, is especially good for this since it offers advice on several of our most important life issues in one easy-to-access location.

You may want to open the book randomly to any page (my personal favorite approach to any book); you might be surprised how divine wisdom guides you to exactly what you most need to hear. Or perhaps you'll choose to go through the book, reading one chapter each day or week.

You may want to try to set aside a specific time each day to meditate and tune into what *your* soul's wisdom has to share about the topic you are currently exploring. You can do this by simply connecting with your breath, softening your heart, and opening to whatever is revealed to you. I also suggest keeping what I call a *Miraculous Moments Journal* to track any synchronistic events, new insights or changes you feel prompted to make during your journey.

## Find Your Own Path

I have no idea how this book will speak to you. All I know is that we each receive guidance in whatever form we are most open to at any given moment. The many ways in which Spirit gets our attention are like a brilliant tapestry — this for you, that for me. The more we awaken to the beauty of this dance being patterned throughout our lives and the uniqueness of our own personal dance step with the divine, the more miraculously our lives flow.

I believe we all have access to a higher energy all the time — whether we view this as Spirit, our higher selves, or simply intuition. All we have to do is turn on the laptop in our life — whatever form that takes for each of us — and make the time and space to honor what we receive.

Follow your heart, trust your instincts and allow yourself to do what feels best. As you embark on your own personal adventure, my greatest wish is that above all, you experience great joy, and trust your wisdom within. This is what *Soul Wisdom* is all about.

# 1

# Miracles

*Miracles are natural, life as it truly is.*

*I slump down into the couch. It's one of those days. I'm tired of working in a job that doesn't fulfill me, and bored with a life that doesn't seem to be going my way.*

"Write."

*I hear a voice. I'm not sure if it's coming from inside my head, outside of me, or if I imagined it. I hear it again.*

"Write."

*On a whim, I pick up my laptop computer, open it and turn it on. The cursor blinks at me expectantly from the blank screen of my word processing program.*

*I hesitate at first, my hands resting lightly on the keys. Then my fingers begin moving as if being led by an outside force.*

You are my child. You are of me. You are made of pure luminescence. You leave me to learn, you return to me when you finish—a circle with no beginning, no end. An ongoing pattern over and over again. It never ends; it never began. It always was.

*What the...?*

You are so beautiful, colorful. You are made of Light, beautiful light—love. You are love in an awkward body so much slower than your true nature. Your true nature travels at the speed of light and beyond.

You laugh. You play. You know what it feels like. You dance. You do that here, on earth. While you walk, your soul soars.

It dances at night and giggles in the morning as you slowly struggle to dress, grappling with the duality of human existence with a soul inside.

The body is essential, important because it slows you down enough to learn your lessons. Because if you were to fly all the time, would you really want to learn? Flying is so much fun, you know.

*"Can you tell me why my life feels so out of control?" I type.*

You pay so much attention to that which is not important—your home, your body, your cars. These are just tools, tools with which to learn. You use them. You choose them.

You need humanness; it's the best solution I've come up with for processing soul lessons. Think of it— you are the most powerful creatures on earth. What lessons that brings with it. What dilemmas! Being human is full of dilemmas and it keeps getting richer.

This—your classroom, the playground, the chalkboard, your human body, the darkness you perceive—all of it is an illusion. This is true because you are one with me. Just as you choose to force your children to go to school, you intuitively know it's sometimes necessary to slow free spirits to help them learn.

Most of your difficulties, you construct. I cannot change what you construct, or I choose not to, because that is my greatest way of showing you my love—free will. That is how you truly love. You set someone free. I have done that to you as an example. As much as it hurts me when I see what you sometimes create, I let you go.

*Do you have any guidance, any advice that could help me right now?*

You write your own journey. I am constantly amazed at what you come up with. I help. Others who know the way, who have used these human tools before, they also help. We all help. We help you in any way we can to give you the easiest path whenever we can.

It amazes me really (chuckling), your lessons keep getting richer, tougher, more challenging. Not bad or good, just fodder for the next souls who pass this way. You're coming up with all kinds of solutions for the human-soul struggle. If only more of you realized you don't need to do it.

The only way I intervene is through guidance. I do not change what is, because the only truth is what you really are—Light, part of me.

You are souls. At night—oh, the adventures you have. You had one just last night, that's right. While you are sleeping, you have adventures. You think they are dreams. But you are talking, working things out. You telecommunicate while you sleep, which is second nature to you, something you do quite well. Talking to the souls you need to, achieving things in split seconds that might take you hours, weeks, years, maybe, to do in your human form. That's recess. Some of the best strides happen at recess.

I intervene by giving you each other, by leading you to things you have created, that others have created, exercises to teach you soul lessons, to teach you the way. You decide whether or not to follow my lead.

## Chapter 1: Miracles

At all times, I always show you the easiest way. The easiest way to learn, heal and remove obstacles. It's all very easy.

What I call easy, you call a miracle. To me, miracles are natural, life as it truly is.

# 2

# Love

*You all achieve miracles because...you are all love.*

**I have many questions, many things I'd like to know.**

Ask, my child.

**Well, you mentioned we are here, on earth, to learn certain lessons. What kind of lessons, exactly?**

You learn to be kind to each other, how to love each other, how to forgive. Those are all human talk—the cloak, you might say, that covers the real intention of human existence: to realize we're all one. I give you a structured environment that feigns non-oneness. I make the incentives to hang onto non-oneness so attractive to see if you truly trust in me.

*A test?*

Not a test the way you are thinking. It's all love. It's like bringing a child to the edge of the sea and letting her explore instead of throwing her in. You let your children skirt the edge—feel the water, let it lap on their toes, then get knocked to their feet from that first big wave. That's what it's about. Letting you experiment, play and feel. Life is a playground.

That's what this human existence of yours is all about. As a people, you're toppling. You're creating more and more challenges. You're fighting yourself. I wanted life to be a testing ground, more like a playground, but this is a bit much. That's why I'm intervening with some of you. I need more of you to understand what it's all about.

*What do you mean, what it's all about?*

Love. You love to view yourselves as separate. Everything you've built is structured on it. Your lesson is not just to understand you are one, but to live it in all you do. Know it within the depth of your heart. Until you have gotten that, you'll keep coming back.

*What do you mean, coming back?*

Back, you know, back to earth.

*Meaning reincarnation?*

Reincarnation for some, past lives for others. Those words tire me (sigh). It's an experience and experiment. It's life. You keep giving children exercises, don't you? You keep teaching them until they get it right. Don't you think I'd give you the same? Once you realize your body is nothing more than a worksheet, once you really understand that, then you'll know.

*What about love?*

Ah, my child, you are so attached to your version of romantic love. Romantic love is what I have created to allow you to come closest on earth to what all of life truly is. Male, female love, romantic love. It's a gift—an easy lesson. Even that lesson isn't so easy for some of you.
    To truly give yourself to another person, to feel the ecstasy of true bliss—that's what it's all about. It's about all forms of love: mother, father love; child, parent love; all forms of truly giving and being present for each other.

I send you in pairs. I send you to find each other. Two parts make a whole. Your lesson is learning how parts fit together like a puzzle, fit together perfectly, you say. And it is perfect, isn't it? Love is perfect. It is all there is. I have chosen to emulate two distinct aspects of myself — female and male, moon and sun, night and day. Most of nature, in humans, in you, is in two distinct pairs. That's the easiest way for you to see how parts make a whole.

Two humans merge and form a new, completely whole human. You have two eyes, two nostrils, two arms, two legs. Night and day make a whole. The exercise of life for you is about the perfection of pairs.

I could have also taught you in fraction, how all the fractionated souls in the whole world create just that — a whole world — but that's not as intimate, as easy to get. I'm looking to make the lesson as easy for you to understand as possible.

All love is sacred because love is all there is. Your life existence is all about love. Love is what it's all about. Love anyone, anyone at all, and you are learning. Love is all that matters. Love is what you are. Two men loving each other, two women loving each other, it is all love. When something is love, that is all there is.

Love of the purest kind is divine. You can experience divinity with anyone; in fact, with everyone is the intention. If it's pure love, it's divine. It doesn't matter who you love because you're all souls. You are all one. We are all one. I want you to love each other.

Chapter 2: Love

Romantic love on earth is the easiest exercise and only the beginning. When you feel deep inner love and see the Light in each person, then you are on your way.

*I'm a bit confused about being separate beings, yet one. Can you say a bit more about that?*

You ask so many questions, my dear. They are part of the mystery that keeps you learning. Just like your left eye is slightly different than your right, and each cell and bit of your skin is unique, so too are all of my children. Yet you are all part of the same body.

*Why is there suffering?*

Every soul, every fractionated part of myself is on a different journey. You choose different exercises, different obstacles to overcome, all of which are blocking you from learning the one true lesson — oneness. There are many different blocks to seeing the one true lesson. You each choose your own way. Some create more suffering; some choose more. You each choose different routes to help one another learn, and to learn yourself.

*Do souls travel together?*

Yes. I send you with other souls with whom you have the greatest magnetization so you increase your chances of learning. In reality, you can learn this lesson with anyone because we are all one.

*So why do we meet specific people? Are there specific souls that are meant to be more significant to us?*

You are given those you're with in your life because those are the ones you have the most to learn from — the ones who can help you the most. Kind of like team learning.

Some of you have been together for so long. I like that. You have learned so much together. It works for you. What isn't broke... (chuckling) you know the expression.

It's like this. You choose different lessons. You get yourself a bit mired up sometimes. Tangled up, in a bit of a snag. You attract those people who can help you the most. I want nothing more than for you to understand your true identity.

*What about soul mates?*

I can't tell you what you want to hear. Some of you are very special to each other. You are not exclusive soul mates. We are all soul mates, my dear. I love you all equally and you are all one.

Soul mates in the way you're saying would mean that some of you are more special than others are. You are all loved equally. And you can love each other equally.

## Chapter 2: Love

Remember, you are fractionated only for the purpose of this exercise. As you learn to love all parts of yourself, you learn to love all your soul mates. Everyone is teaching you so much, and everyone is growing with you—don't you see? As you learn, your teachers change with you. They become different teachers in the same bodies. You have chosen a powerful group of parts with which to travel.

**What is a miracle?**

A miracle is life as it is meant to be. A miracle is love.

**Can we all achieve miracles?**

You all achieve miracles because you are all miracle workers. You are all love.

# 3

# Health

*They believed so completely, it made them well.*

**What about health?**

Your body <u>is</u> your lesson. The biggest lesson there is. Your body is your complete worksheet. You practice; you remove obstacles. Some of you with chronic diseases catapult through lessons like there's no tomorrow.
    Your body is more than your physical body. Your body is the house for all the emotions you experience. It's your thoughts, subconscious and conscious. It's so much

more complex than any of you realize or will ever understand.

You're trying. I like that. The study of the body, the human experience—whether it's studying the physical body through medicine, psychology, nutrition, energy work, spirituality—this is good. When you study who you are, it helps. It helps so much. It gives those who haven't studied their bodies some framework to work within. You'll never fully understand it because that's the idea, but keep trying.

Your body—all aspects of it—is so complex because it is the worksheet for your soul experience. Nature is the experience and the experiment, the playground in which you learn. And it's a good school indeed.

*Are you saying disease is good?*

What most of you don't realize is these things you call illnesses or dis-ease are gifts. Physical weaknesses are like power buttons, triggers to remind you to learn what you're here to learn. Good, bad, black, white. It's not a judgment thing. It just is. What you think is good or bad is just a learning mechanism.

*Meaning?*

Soul lessons. Your physical symptoms reign you in to learn what you are ready to learn. The more open you are

Chapter 3: Health

to receiving the gifts your body has to offer, the more you can heal its weaknesses as well.

Sometimes physical symptoms mean you need time, time to heal. A lot can happen just by being.

**Is all learning done through illness and healing?**

It's one way—a rudimentary way many of you have chosen. There are other ways. Violence. Some of you have chosen the most barren ways to return to help others. You have chosen war, violence, destruction. These are not the best ways to teach or to learn, but they are ways.

I love you so I want your learning experience to be as loving and easy as possible. And it can be. You know that. Any child knows learning can be fun, exciting and wonderful.

You forget sometimes you are learning and get caught in the lesson, going over the same spot again and again instead of moving forward. It's like a bear looking for berries that spends all his energy focusing on the briar patch, getting more and more snarled instead of remembering to move to the next patch to get more berries.

Life can be so easy. I want you to choose the way that flows. Sometimes that's not what you want. You want to go in circles or to suffer because of some human construct you believe. It's difficult to watch and not what I would choose, but I won't take choice away from you. That's love.

*So how do people heal?*

You can heal by understanding, believing, accepting and living even for a moment your own oneness. When you accept you are in a state of oneness, you are healing. Love is all it takes to heal.

All the suffering can be over completely. That's what Jesus was all about. Jesus taught you that you can heal. No struggle. In a second. The people Jesus healed in the Bible believed completely. Completely. They got it. They understood oneness. They had faith. Not an ounce of doubt. They believed so completely, it made them well. You can do that.

*A lot of people truly want to heal themselves but they still die.*

Do they? Do they want to heal? Do they believe? Sometimes healing means completely transforming everything you believe to be true. Changing your mind. Sometimes the cost of giving up what you believe is too great—or you think it is—compared to healing.

You want to heal, but you want to believe that you are separate, different. You want to believe that everything that you think is true is. Healing means recognizing the world is quite different than you thought it to be.

You can live forever. You can teach. You can heal. The things you want most in life and receive don't matter. They are all a lesson. Life teaches miracles happen. What

Chapter 3: Health

you put in your mind happens. You create what you think.

If you believe and truly trust that something is guiding you, you will be guided. In so many small, mundane ways, I have served you up miracles on a silver platter. Accepting the miracles in your life can be as easy as you want.

And sometimes dying is healing.

*What happens when we die?*

When you die, I send spirits whom I know you will feel oneness with, a connection—love. You'll remember the love you experienced with them when they were people on earth and that will help you make the transition to love with me more easily.

I have been told it's the deepest feeling of love and happiness, infinite times better than what you feel on earth. I wouldn't know. It's all I know. It's all I am.

*What if we don't choose love?*

Then you choose the shadow instead. It doesn't matter. You cannot change the truth in your choosing. You can only change your perception of the truth. You cannot change what already is so.

*I've always believed that when we die we become one with God. Is that true?*

(Chuckling.) That's funny. I've always believed you were already one with me.

# 4

# Spirit

*I am what I am. I am Light. I am Love.*
*I am everything and everyone. I am One.*

**How can I change my life?**

Trust. I hear you listening. I know you hear. Yet you are caught up in the farce.
 Life as you know it is a game, an exercise. I know you understand. Yet you chose to stay stuck.
 When you turn the other way, you turn your back on me, your ultimate lover. I am your soul mate. You know this yet you chose to stay where you are out of fear.

You are attached, attached to the constraints of human life. All of this will be erased like chalk on the board. The house, the money, the body, the friends and loved ones as they look and are right now.

They may be with you the next time and even the next, but they will not look the same way. You are attached to that which doesn't matter. You get the lessons but you don't move on.

I have chosen so many messengers all over the world. I am planting seeds. Just as humans have developed technology, you have also developed new ways to communicate with me. Or returned to old ways, just modified them. It's an era of communication.

*Are specific people chosen to communicate?*

You are all chosen. Anyone who wants the job can have it (laughing). None of you are more special than the next. You are all equally special. That's what you will tell your children. It's important for you to help each other see the Light, to remember what you are.

*What do you mean, remember?*

You are never sent to earth again unless you remember me in between. You can't. You must become one with your mother before she can give birth.

## Chapter 4: Spirit

*Are you female?*

My child (laughing hard). I know you know the answer to that. I am neither. Men are not more god-like than women just like women are not more god-like than men. You are both of the Light; you are all of the Light. I gave you both. I gave you it all.

    I am like female. I am like male. Everything that you are is everything that I am. I am everything positive. I am the peaceful stillness of a moonlit night, the glory of a sunbeam bright. I am the first step on a snowdrift sight, the smell in spring delight. I am what I am. I am Light. I am Love. I am everything and everyone. I am One.

    You are male, female, tall and short; you are all of it just like I am. Look at every culture, every person—everything good in them is everything good in you. Until you all—fractionated souls—choose love, the human experience will continue.

*I receive these words, but I'm still doubtful. Are these words really coming from a source outside of me, from you? Are you God?*

Your question tells me you are slow in learning. There is no source outside of you. I am what I am. You are part of me. You are God. God is you. We are One. These words come from the source of you that is Spirit. When the words come from a source other than Spirit, you will know.

*Many religions refer to "God within." Is that what you are referring to?*

That is right. That is the one true message.

*So when we pray, aren't we seeking a God outside of ourselves?*

I don't know. Are you? When you pray, pray as if you are the stomach of the body. Pray to remind yourself you are connected to all others. When you pray, pray to all the other organs, pray to remind them who they are and to remind yourself who you are.

Pray to the whole body, the One True Source that houses you, constantly regenerating you and providing refuge — the you who is so much greater than who you are alone. Pray to the source to keep providing shelter, movement and life. Pray for direction so you can continue fulfilling your purpose.

*What is my purpose?*

Your life is about playing, enjoying, relishing in all the gifts of life I have given you — gifts of nature, gifts of beauty, gifts of each other. In relishing my gifts, you see how much I love you. You learn and remember love.

As you play, remind each other Who You Are through right action. Love each other, love yourself. Because as you love and forgive and are graceful with yourself, so too are you with one another. This will save you.

**You mention 'being saved.' What do you mean by that?**

Remembering. Returning to me. Re-entering the womb.

# 5

# Shadow

*How else is there to teach about Light,
but to also offer the dark?*

**Are there spirits other than you?**

The shadow. You have finally begun to understand the shadow. I am pleased. That is a major step in your learning, my child. You are infinitely creative. Now you can truly begin to heal. I am all there is. But the shadow is also true.

*Is the shadow the devil?*

The devil as you describe it is the shadow within each of you. Some people chose to let the shadow take over them. It is a choice. I never force myself on anyone. Exploring the shadow is part of life's lesson. I made it so. Without darkness, there is no light. Without Light, no darkness. The shadow is the darkness in your own heart. Without me, it would not exist.

You never go to the darkness or let the shadow engulf your heart without your choice. You are *always* with me. Even those who are in darkness, I love and am with. They are with me. They just believe that they are not.

**What is the shadow?**

The shadow is whatever you choose to believe other than that you are totally lovable. It's what you choose to create as a result of that belief.

Some people choose to say negative things, to create illness in their bodies to attract love. The options are endless. The shadow is whatever you choose to do to keep yourself busy instead of loving. The shadow is everything you do to keep love when you have forgotten you already have all the love that you need.

You are all seeking love from each other, from yourself, from anywhere. This is your greatest struggle, the greatest irony.

Oh, the bliss, the ecstasy I see you all experience when you realize the truth, when you join us even in those moments in your dreams. You each seek happiness in so many different ways—food, drink, sex, drugs, exercise. The euphoria you experience with these is only 1/100th or less than the euphoria you experience when you recognize you are really Light beings.

**How do we recognize them Light from the dark if we aren't supposed to judge?**

Just as there is a speck of darkness in the light to remind you what lightness is, so too it is in your hearts. Your job is to identify your own darkness, and say, "Ah, yes, there it is."
Judge not. Recognize, yes. Judge, no. When you see something that is not love, detach from it. By judging, you are so engaged in the fact that darkness is "other"—other than yourself—you are saying that you have none. That is not your job.
When you see darkness in another, the only thing to do is to say to yourself, "Ah, yes, I recognize that. That is darkness. That is shadow. I recognize that because that is in me too."
The darkness is like all else. It is a learning tool—nothing more, nothing less. Look at it as such. Its only purpose is to guide you to the Light again.
When you see the darkness, think, "Ah, so if that is darkness, then this is Light. The Light is what I go to, not

darkness." And so, the shadow has played its part in the teaching exercise. You see how powerful it is?

So many of you get caught up in the darkness for the sake of darkness, the ups and downs of darkness, the roller coaster slopes of darkness, the shades of dark. Yours is not to learn the essence of darkness just as yours is not to learn the essence of Light.

*We're taught so many rules—don't lie, don't kill, don't cheat —what about the ten commandments?*

There is only one commandment. Love each other as you love yourself as I love you and you love me. The end.

*What about the other commandments?*

At times when you've been stuck, I've offered words just as I'm offering words right now—words that I thought would help. Words to ease your pain, make things clearer, help you understand.

Never before have I been so clear as when I gave you Jesus. The other commandments, they are all good. The ten commandments, you see, are subsets of the one true commandment. They mean the same thing. If you are doing the one true commandment, you do the others as well. I give you what you need when you need it.

*What about keeping a Sabbath?*

Chapter 5: Shadow

I want you to remember me. The Sabbath is a way you remember. Remember what I said about the playground? I want it to be easy. I want us to play together. Worshiping is one way we do that.

Meditating, dreaming, playing, singing, dancing — worship in any form is a way you love me as yourself. People have so many different ways they do that and they're all good.

**What about guilt?**

Why would you ever feel guilty for being what you are? You are what you are just like I am what I am. The rest is illusion. It's all human noise, distractions keeping you from getting on with your learning. If you believe someone else can make you feel guilty then you believe someone else has more power than you, power over you. They don't. No one has power over you and you don't have power over anyone because we are all the same.

**Wow.**

Don't you see, saying one of you has power over another one of you is like saying that one cell has power over another, one drop of blood can control the next. It's impossible. Domination is the oldest game in the book, the game that keeps you from realizing your truth the most.

Your Spirit is as infinite as I am. You will always exist. Your body can bleed, but there is no wound, no dent, no tarnish on you—your true self, because your body is a teaching tool.

You are all completely and utterly equal—all ages, all sizes, all races, both genders. Until you all learn this, there will be more work to do.

**What about Hitler?**

Hitler helped many of you recognize the shadow in yourselves. Hitler could have chosen to embrace the Light, just like so many of you can. He did not. His is the way not to choose.

He is still of the Light. He is still in the Light. He was a misguided soul who was given free will as I give you all free will. He chose to play with fire.

Don't kid yourself that no Hitlers are now on the earth. There are plenty and they are all my children, all Light with specks of darkness. They choose to go deep into the shadows. They have chosen difficult lessons and have gotten lost on the way. They have forgotten Who They Are.

Many who died learned how to be fully with the Light in dying. They learned forgiveness. They recognized the shadow in their perpetrators as the same shadow in themselves, and they saw Light in the darkness of other.

How else is there to teach about Light, but to also offer the dark?

## Chapter 5: Shadow

*Does the shadow take over people?*

No one gets taken over by the shadow. They choose it. No one in the shadow is trapped. They can turn away as quickly as they came. Within what you would say a millisecond, they can be whole, one with me and totally in the Light. A miracle you would say. I would say, As It Is.

**What about hell?**

It is hell when you don't learn well enough, isn't it? That can hurt. It is hell when you don't believe you are in the Light. When you hurt others, you in turn get hurt. And that can be hell.

**What will happen when we all choose the Light?**

It will be bliss.

# 6

# Spiritual Sight

*You can rise up in this moment and completely change your life with every decision you make.*

**Can you say more about this all being an illusion?**

Remember when you were acting in a play? There were props, costumes, makeup on your face, music in the pit—all that was fake, wasn't it? It appeared to be true. If you let your eyes get unfocused and yourself escape into the adventure of it all, you could almost for a moment believe it was true.

Maybe you really would, for a split second, believe you were the character you were playing. You call that good acting. I call it your life.

*So, if we're not really the characters we are playing, who are we?*

You are beings of Light. Your costumes, your human bodies, the homes you live in—these can conceal your true identity if you choose to let them.

You have so much more fun when you see yourselves as Light beings.

*So, you are saying we create what we look like?*

You create it all. That's the fun of it. I put you on earth when you are ready to learn. You and I, we decide together who you will be with—who your parents will be, who you will travel with. It's all choice. I send you on your way with the help of the others and then the game begins.

You decide how your voice sounds, how you look, how your cells mutate or grow. You decide what diseases you get or resist. You decide your every action, every inch of your appearance, every thing that happens to you. You decide to go left or right on your path. Everything of you, you choose. You may not choose who else is on the path with you because my other children also choose what path they go on. But you decide how you will respond to them. Will you walk closer, hold their hand, turn away? It's all your choice.

**What if we don't like what we've chosen?**

You choose again. Every second of your life you have the opportunity to redo. That's what life is all about. At any given moment, you can change it all. You can't change what you've chosen up to that moment, but you can choose how you view it. You can choose the impact your memories have on your body. Right now, at this millisecond, you can choose to do it all differently. In one second. You have the complete power to do that.

You can talk differently, walk differently, love others completely, slow down, change your appearance, cells and voice. You can choose to flow with positive energy in your homes and bodies. You can choose to follow or lead. You can choose how deeply to breathe, what to look at, how to interpret what you see, how to perceive. You can rise up in this moment and completely change your life with every decision you make.

**If we can do all that, why are so many of us dying, experiencing disease, hurting each other?**

Exactly.

**Huh?**

You're learning. Everyone has this ability. And everyone knows it. Some of you have trouble remembering what you know, trusting what you know.

*I would think lots of people would want to believe that they are Godlike.*

What many people believe is "God" isn't. Do you define God as more powerful than anyone else? If you choose to believe that, you will not heal. Because the idea that you can be more powerful than another person is an illusion.

*Do you mean we can access everything you know?*

You struggle over minuscule decisions. You can overcome the struggling in a heartbeat. There is no reason to analyze, debate or consider because all the answers are available to you.

You have the world's wisdom within. Some of you call this intuition. You are amazed and impressed when one of you demonstrates what you call psychic abilities. I call that Spiritual Sight.

Intuition and psychic abilities are what happen when you look through the eyes and wisdom of Spirit instead of the eyes on your head.

Seeing other dimensions does not make you special. It is something everyone can do. When you see, access, speak from, listen to and feel your own Light within, you will receive the answers you need.

You can see into lands beyond, stories and times untold. You can see the magic within each other's eyes. You can do all this and more. You are each completely capable of achieving miracles in your life. Healing isn't miraculous. Healing is being exactly what you are — completely whole, completely spiritual, completely of the Light.

Only when you interpret this wisdom by way of the shadows can you go astray. The answers will be expressed to each of you in different ways. That is the mystery, the miracle that enables you each to learn so well from each other. When I deliver the message in many different ways, more of you can understand. So I speak in many tongues. Your spiritual language may be different from the next person's, but it all has the same meaning.

When you open your eyes with Spiritual Sight, you can make the waters split; you can heal your own body. Whatever one of my children can do — yes, that includes Jesus — so too can you. That is the message. Everything is possible through the Light.

Perhaps you are scared to hear this because it's a huge responsibility. If you really believed you could make that much of a difference — heal each other, put each other out of misery, completely regenerate your own body, would you live your life the way you are now?

What if you died and on your deathbed looked back and realized you had Spiritual Sight your whole life? What would you regret? What would you wish you had done differently? You might want to think about this, because I promise this will happen to you.

*I hear what you're saying, but I feel like I don't know how to do all these things.*

You each have a unique language written in the center of your heart. It's imbedded on your soul, your secret formula, and you have the key. Stop looking "out there" for answers. Because you have the answers within yourself.

At certain times in your life, I have given you each a secret, an epiphany, something you may not have shared with others. You will remember it as having been a moment of intense and complete joy.

It may have been as a child, it often is. It's when you realize the beauty of life, when you're floating on "cloud nine" and are happier than you've ever been. It's often a moment, a split second where everything may slow down. It may last only a second, an infinitesimal moment.

Look to that moment. Therein lies your own formula for seeing through the eyes of Spirit. You will know when you are seeing the world as Spirit, because you will recognize that feeling of joy.

# 7
# Self Love

*True saints...are those who worship*
*me in themselves.*

**Someone recently told me I let people get away with too much. I think I do this because I want people to like me.**

That's the stuff of it, isn't it?

**What?**

You are finding the one core issue you all have. You think you can be abandoned. You don't realize you are never alone. We are always with each other. You are always with the everlasting presence that never abandons. It's impossible to be left because you are always with.

Telling yourself stories is a way you keep yourself trapped. All the negative things you tell yourself and each other keep you busy, off your one true path. You are now ready to learn the practice of mind control.

*Mind control?*

Yes. To keep pace with your own inner growth and journey, you must know how to control your mind.

*How do I control my mind?*

It's all about focus. You must choose the thoughts that you allow to come into your mind. You have been too lenient with yourself. It is now time to take your goals seriously. Do not tell yourself things that will distract you. The only true thoughts, true path, true decisions are discovered by going within. When you are in the quiet, calm within, then you are one with Spirit.

Eventually, you will always be in this state, you will always act from this haven. This haven and who you are in the world will be the same. It is from this peaceful inner place you must act.

## Chapter 7: Self Love

You need to be gentle with yourself. When you are hard on yourself, you are hard on others. What you need most to learn is how to love yourself. When you are awful to yourself, you are awful to me also, to those you love, those with whom you are deeply connected. I want you to be in a state of complete and pure bliss. The only way to do this is to love yourself. When you learn to do this, really do this, you will be closest to me.

The saints in the world, the true saints, those who have mastered what it is to be alive, are those who worship me in themselves. Your work always starts at home, in your house, your heart.

Your body is your home. It is where you do your lessons, where you learn, where you discover me. My deepest prayer for you is that you learn to care for yourself. Love yourself, be kind to yourself, do not think about what you have not done well but instead, of that which you have.

What you focus on becomes truth for you. In controlling your mind, I mean focusing your mind on the good—think happy thoughts; focus on the positive. Focusing your mind means thinking at all times about the beauty. I have filled this world with beautiful things— find them, focus on them.

True mind control is about allowing yourself to slip into the natural state of utter ecstasy that comes from being with me. When you are one with me, you dance, float, play— all while being unaware that you do these things because you are living in your natural state. You are my children. Treat yourself as kindly in each moment as you would treat me. We are one in the same, you and I. I want to teach you to fly.

**So teach me.**

Lean back. Close your eyes. Imagine a series of beautiful thoughts—everything in this world that means beauty to you. Imagine the center of an iris, the heart of a clover, the soul of a raindrop. Imagine the spray of the sea, each molecule within the spray as it hits your face. Imagine the greatest beauty you have laid eyes on—a mountain, a feather—each piece different than the rest.
    When you dwell on each beautiful moment, seeing into the soul of each fragile element that is life, feeling it with all your soul—know that the beauty you perceive is the beauty of you.

**It's hard for me to believe that about myself. I see all my imperfections. I can be very hard on myself.**

I am going to teach you that imperfection is perfection. What are you judging perfection on? What is perfection? According to whose standards? When did you designate yourself as knowing what is perfect and what is not?
    So many of you have assigned new value to things. Where you came up with these things, I'll never know. The perfect face, the perfect body—what are these things? Who made you judge? I have created all that you lay your

eyes on—all creations of life are of me. Anytime you label or judge another person or being, you also judge me.

The child born with defects, crooked face, body—all of this is perfect. The beautiful model who chose plastic surgery to create a "perfect" face was more perfect before she chose the chisel. This is because her face was an act of God, an act of me.

You cannot take away your own inner perfection by anything you say or do. That is not possible. You cannot improve upon yourself because anything perfect cannot be improved.

Accept what you truly are. You are a child of God. You are perfect unto me. You *are* me. Remember this and focus your skills on remembering that, not erasing that which I have given you.

Look upon that part of yourself you like the least—which you have labeled as "less than." For you, it may not be visual; it may be your limitations in some area—whatever it is—hold it out for me to see.

Really look at it. Cherish that imperfection as if it were a beautiful flower. See how perfectly it is formed. What is unique about it? Recognize how it is different today than it was yesterday.

Every cell in your body is different in this moment than the moment before. Marvel at that miracle. Marvel at the miracle of your blemish. If it's a birthmark, marvel at how in the creation of a human being with multiple cells coming together in love to perfectly form a human being, something special happened to remind you again how perfectly unique you are.

If it is an inner weakness, marvel at how you are always changing. Look into the heart of your imperfection as if it is the heart of a flower bloom, always changing, moving, evolving and growing. That is you, the ultimate beauty of you. Remember there is beauty and perfection in every tiny element that you call "imperfect." As you see the beauty in everything about you, see it even in that part within you that you may have wanted to change, to erase.

Love that part of you, dwell in that part of you; focus on it. Love it like a child who just does not yet understand. Hold it close. Know that any part of you that does not yet understand your perfection is to be cherished, shown the Light. When you shine Light directly on a shadow, it disappears.

Your task in life is to accept that the most beautiful among us and the perfection in all things are also in you. Only then will you fully love me.

**This sounds like a lot of work.**

Fighting your own perfection is a lot of work. Perfection is simple. It is simply being. When you accept what you are, life is simple.

# 8

# Mission

*Your main purpose is to remember what you are.*
*... You are joy.*

**What am I supposed to learn today?**

I want to tell you to enjoy your life's mission. Really enjoy it. And remember what it is. You all have one. For some of you, it is just to talk and share with an older neighbor. For others, it's to be a good parent or friend. For others, it's to make another's load a bit lighter. For some of you, it's to tell the truth in your heart in so many different ways, maybe to paint or teach.

Find your mission. For some, it is learning love through the art of gardening or working with wood. Find your passion. It is a day-to-day way of living. It matters not what you do. And you fool yourself if you pretend that it is about "saving" others. You help others when you remind them what they are by what you do. They are God. Light. Love. One with you.

Your mission is not about saving others. It is always about saving yourself. Healing yourself. Learning to love. Learning to become One. Healing yourself always involves healing others. But that is not your main purpose.

Your main purpose is to remember what you are. You are God. You are one with God. You are Light. You are music. You are laughter. You are joy. You are happiness. You are nature. You are one with the beauty of the earth.

Your life mission does not have to be grandiose. In fact, it never is. That is not your true life mission. Your true life mission is loving each other with all your heart, loving others as the same as God. You are each meant to do this in slightly a different way. But the goal is always the same.

Your mission is always about reminding others who they are. There is only one way to do this — remembering it yourself.

# 9

# Present Moment

*How much of your life is lost because you act as if you are the same person you were a few moments ago?*

**What you describe sounds wonderful. But is it really possible to live like this?**

You need to know everything that you've ever wanted may no longer be who you are. Everything you think is important is not. Everything you desire is taking you away from the one true intention of your life — to begin again.

There are a lot of reasons for this, but the most fitting is that you are remembering things that don't exist. You're dwelling in the past. You are forgetting the one true message—what is passed away is gone, truly gone. All that went before is no longer here. It doesn't exist.

**But if there's no time, doesn't everything from the past and future lie here?**

The only reason for having time is to give you a perspective on where you've come. Everything you are not proud of and everything that you are, let it go. It no longer exists.

**I don't think I understand.**

Nothing is as important as what is right now, where you are right now. Nothing is as important because nothing else is true. The only truth is in this second, and that is passed. What you were before in your humanness is no more. You are not there, you are here. Be here rather than looking over your shoulder to see what came before.

**I understand what you're saying, but the whole idea of the past being gone forever kind of blows my mind.**

How much of your life is lost because you act as if you are the same person you were a few moments ago? That is the

## Chapter 9: Present Moment

real beauty of the message. You are the child, the one who is constantly being reborn, rebuilt.

You can be brand new. You don't need to be who you once were. You don't need to focus on who that was. All that was before is already gone. Acting "as if" doesn't make it more gone. It already is.

The truth is that what has gone before has passed away. It no longer exists. It is forgotten. It is forgiven. You can't go back in time and you don't want to. You can't go forward. That is the real blessing of this experiment called time. There is the present moment and the present moment is only love.

Every single moment of every single day you are given a new opportunity to realize you are what I see you as, a new being with no shackles. You are free, you are now, you are born anew, and you are nothing but a child of love.

Begin again in a state of reverence, awe and gratitude for what you are, and for the graciousness of my gift to you. All is well.

# 10

# Words To Live By

*Whenever there is stillness, there I am.*

**Can you offer me some guidance I can use in my everyday life?**

Consult the Light before each and every thing you do, phone call you make, person you hug. Always be mindful. I am always directing you. Answers are available for every decision in life. They are all equally significant. Every word you speak, action you take, thing you say—however minor it seems—all of it is important to me.

My message lies deep within and is yours for the taking. At any moment when you feel lost, there is nothing to do to find your way. Simply turn to that which you already are.

Just like a crow searches among the ravaged bits for a treasure, so too I search among you all. I cull through the shadow to find the bits that are less ravaged, the parts of you ready to recognize what you are.

Every time you resist that which flows in your life, I will be there. Trust me. I will deliver the truth to you in love. All you have to do is listen.

*I hear these words, yet I struggle to put them into practice.*

Here are some words to live by.

## On Wealth

Remember that the only true wealth lies within. The Light offers gems worth more than anything you can imagine in the illusion of the world. Be not attached to material objects. They are an exercise only, to remind yourself what you are. The less you are attached to worldly goods, whatever the kind, the more you will receive the wealth of the universe in all its forms. By letting go of that which is not, you will gain all that is.

The more you recognize that material objects don't matter, the more wealth will flow into your life. When

## Chapter 10: Words To Live By

you let go of the illusion that material possessions are part of you—your identity—only then will you receive the abundance that wholeness brings.

The only true wealth is within; you already have it. The more you accept how wealthy you are already are since you are a child of God, the more you will feel this abundance. No matter how much money you have on earth, you are all equally wealthy, you are all completely rich. No increase in money can make you more so; no earthly lack makes you less so. All you truly need lies within.

Accept your divine richness and know that just like physical illness, any dips or increases in your earthly wealth are all exercises in divine seeing. It's all an illusion, an opportunity to remind you of the wealth that is already yours. Even those among you who are without clothes, food or health are still just as wealthy as all the rest because your wealth lies with me.

If you recognize that your worldly goods are an illusion—play money—then also remember that anytime you can put even one of my children out of their misery, you do the same to me. Remember that true wealth doesn't lie in your wallet or bank, but in your soul. It is already yours.

You are infinitely unique and the same as all others. That is why there are no two humans, snowflakes, trees, anything exactly alike. I show you through your uniqueness how infinite the wealth of the universe is. We will never run out of unique combinations, so great is the bank of our choices. Your wealth is infinite.

## On Personal Relationships

Remember that most problems in relationships stem from the one simple mistake of seeing other people as separate from you. Nothing anyone can say or do can take away your worth, just as nothing you can say or do can increase it. You are divine, you are of the Light. You are my child. Nothing will ever change that, not death, not the shadow, not sin. The minute you accept this, you will be able to fully love another without getting caught up in earthly matters.

Matters of control are silly. No one can ever control you or belittle you unless you choose to accept that the illusion is true. The minute you are aligned with the truth of heaven, all earthly conflict will disappear because you will know you are One.

## On Career

Know that the work you choose to do in the world does not matter. Career does not give you value. Your value was already determined before your birth. It is unchangeable and the same as all others. Your job is to look inward, to see your Oneness, your Light, and make all decisions based on being in the Light. All decisions are to be made of love because there is nothing else. If anything other than love prompts you, that is not the right decision. It's that simple. Know that all that you ask for, as long as it is of love, is yours. What you truly want in heaven you will have.

## On Children

Teach children that they are of the Light. That is your only task. You teach a child more by example than by words. If you treat each other and children as if they are the equals that they are — as God-beings — with deep reverence, respect and love, you will have done well.

If you live a life of simplicity, joy and love, you will teach children to do the same. If at all times, you strive to align yourself with me and with the Light in others; if at all times, you accept this and nothing else to be the truth, then you will teach children all they need to know.

This is true for children of all ages. You teach so much more by not speaking at all. For in the tranquility of your silence, you allow the Light to speak. That is a language everyone understands. Notice at all times what you are saying without your words.

Love is in the silence. Teach children to listen to the wisdom within their own souls by being quiet in Love. Trust that all this and more is true. Remind children who they are. Show them this in everything you do and say. All children of the world are all of the Light. Believe this and show them this in how you treat them, how you treat yourself and how you treat all the people of the earth.

## On The Environment

The entire living earth is mine, of the Light and part of me. The earth is my gift to my children to have and enjoy. Every living being is to be cherished. Sometimes it is easier to see the Light in another human being or within yourself than in the trees you use for wood and the animals you use for meat. It is all of me. If you are to use any of it, do so with reverence, love and respect.

Every interaction with everything of the earth is an opportunity to help you remember. Be reverent and thankful for that which you have. If you honor the Light in people and not in other living things, you are still in darkness. Remember, the system I gave you in the beginning is far too perfect ever to be understood by earthly minds. Nothing of God ever needs to be perfected.

## On Guilt or Error

Remember that nothing exists but love. Your errors and sins disappear for me the moment they occur. There is only love. That is what forgiveness is. The moment you recognize that what you have done is not of love and you want to do differently, that is all the seed you need to be forgiven. Every interaction with darkness is an opportunity to seek the Light. I don't want you to suffer. By staying stuck in the past, by revisiting your mistakes, by reveling in regret or allowing yourself to feel guilty, you miss opportunities to shine your Light.

By keeping yourself busy with judgment and sorrow, you are choosing to resist the Light. Turn away from these belabored actions. You are exhausting yourself and others. You are perpetuating the darkness and missing important opportunities to begin again. Begin again in this moment and know you are already forgiven. Do the same for your brothers and sisters. Know that just as I have forgiven you, so too can you forgive others and yourself.

## On Judgment

Anything you do to one of my children, you do to all of my children including yourself. Remember anytime you call one of my children useless, stupid, evil, careless or anything less than divine, you call me the same.

When you act as if you are wiser than God, as if you know someone's worth, you make a grave and careless error. No child of mine is anything other than Light. You may act out of false perceptions, you may choose actions that are other than love, but you are always love. The only thing you can do is to recognize when someone acts from the shadow, so you can recognize the shadow within yourself, and choose love instead.

Remember each person is on his or her own journey and path. I reveal completely unique opportunities to each person for restoring sight. That is another example of the infinite wealth of the Light that you are part of, endless learning opportunities. If you think someone else is choosing wrongly, look at how you may be choosing wrongly by perceiving that person as other than completely perfect. The minute you judge a person rather than their actions, you are in darkness.

The shadow you see in another is the shadow in yourself. Use this perception as an opportunity to separate out your own darkness and recognize your own Light.

## When You See Yourself Judging Someone

Stop, and do the following.

1) Thank that person silently for revealing a learning opportunity to you. Think of how you have done the same thing as this person or may be doing the same right now (by choosing something other than love).

2) Envision that person in the Light, completely perfect and part of me.

3) Pray for your Spiritual Sight to be restored and guidance in choosing love in all things.

## When You See Another Person Judging You

Know that their judgements are not truth. How quickly you cloud your vision by paying attention to the criticism

## Chapter 10: Words To Live By

of others. Instead, criticism is others' fear and ignorance talking. Be not afraid or angry with those who judge; be compassionate. For you are them, and they are you. Their fear is your fear; their choice to stay in the shadow is from fear and anxiety, not evil. As Jesus said, "Forgive them, for they know not what they do."

Be not callous but let their comments, anything that is not love, bounce off your armor like the ding of a willow branch, soft and limber. Trust only that which you know. Waste no time or energy engaging with anything that is not love. Instead, spend your energy getting to know the depth of others' souls that is Spirit.

## On Physical Pain or Illness

Trust that you are not your body. Your body is a gift, a lesson, a worksheet. You practice your lessons on your body and learn well from it. Be grateful to your body for teaching you so well. When your body is calling out to you, thank it. Thank your body for telling you that something is not well in your perception. Be grateful to your body for giving you yet another opportunity for learning. Sometimes your body shouts the loudest when the greatest opportunity is nigh. Seize the opportunity and learn your lessons well.

If you are working out something on the worksheet you call body, remember, it is only a tool for helping you to restore your Spiritual Sight. Disease does not change who you are, it only reminds you that you are so much more than a physical self. Be grateful to discomfort for guiding you to restore your Sight.

## On Dying

You are always alive, always with me, always well. It has never been otherwise. Even when my children pass away from this earth, they are always with me. Sometimes, the greatest healing happens in death. For then, your earthly perceptions pass away and you can see clearly that you are one with me.

Disease can mean you are on the verge of discovering this reality. You may achieve it in dying, or in living, but either way you will realize the full magnitude of what it means to be alive.

Choose not to be sad when someone has died. Be happy and know they are with me, and are also still with you. When you die, you do not leave the earthly plane, you are simply allowed to exist without the earthly burdens that make Spiritual Sight less easy.

In dying, you will experience the great joy that comes from being with Spirit and with all others at the same time. Imagine the great joy you will experience when you realize and accept the glory of this!

Chapter 10: Words To Live By

## On Natural Disasters

Know that these are all an illusion, a teaching exercise to help you return to me. Natural disasters teach so much about love. Anything that offers an opportunity for you to recognize that you are Spirit is helpful.

Many disasters that you deem natural are really consequences of free will, the free will my children have taken over hundreds of years.

To say they are punishments is to be completely misguided. I do not punish my children. That would serve no purpose. Instead there are infinite opportunities to help you to see. That is what I want more than anything — I want you each to see and live what you are — Love.

## On Fear

Know that there is nothing to fear. Fear itself does not exist; it is something you constructed and designed. What is there to be afraid of, if you cannot die or disappear; what is there to fear if you are always with those you love and always will be, if you are always with me and always will be?

Even if you are afraid of losing the self you mistakenly think you have constructed, even if you are afraid of losing your individuality, you will realize this is silly once you understand that you are one with the most powerful being in the universe. That will never be taken away from you.

When you are afraid, say: "**I am one with the Light; God and all others are always with me. I live forever as God does; I am pure divine Light. In my divinity, I am whole, love, and will always be.**"

## On Love

Love is seeing all that is good in others and if your eyes are closed to it, trusting still that it is there. Love is living your oneness. To learn to love, act as if everything you know within the depths of your heart is true: You are God's child and so are your brother and sister. We are all One. Love is living as if this is true.

## On Knowing God

Let yourself be silent, for in the silence you hear me. Whenever there is silence, there is the opportunity to know the Light. I am in the spaces between the words you speak.

Let yourself look into another person's eyes, for there you will see me. Really look. Really see. Let those you meet know that you see me in them. Let yourself be still, for when you stop all action, you will feel me. Whenever there is stillness, there I am.

Chapter 10: Words To Live By

## Seven Steps To Manifesting Change

1. **See your shadow.** Really look for it, become aware, accept that the shadow exists and is part of the human experience.

2. **Recognize that the shadow in others is only a learning opportunity.** When you see fault in another's actions, allow your vision to be open to how you have made the same choices you now criticize.

3. **Pause and be silent.** Recognize that silence and peace provide an opportunity for you to go inside, close out the distractions of the earthly illusions and see the Light within. Seek silence and solitude several times each day.

4. **Recognize your own Light.** Allow your Light to be visible to you. Practice seeing yourself as the bright and shining Light you are.

5. **Let your Light shine out to the world.** When you see, speak, hear and feel from the Light within, others will recognize it and be glad.

6. **Seek answers.** Ask for help and it shall be given. Know all the help you need lies within. Seek the answers and trust you already know and have all you need.

7. **Honor the whole.** Be grateful and joyful that you are part of the whole. Recognize you are One.

# Eight Steps to Activating Miracles

1. **Breathe.** Breath is your connection to the breath of the Light.

2. **Envision.** Imagine a beautiful calm Light surrounding your whole body in protection and safety.

3. **Root.** Imagine red energy roots flowing from your feet and connecting you to the core of the earth.

4. **Float.** Envision a purple light flowing from the heavens into the crown of your head connecting you to the larger whole.

5. **Speak.** Say to yourself, "I am what I am what I am. I am of the Light. I bask in the Light of all others."

6. **Pray.** Be grateful for what you have and all that is.

7. **Love.** See others as Light beings. Recognize the Light shining from their eyes. Say nothing, just bask in their Light and allow your own to shine out to them.

8. **Act.** Act of the Light, in the Light, through the Light. Be all that you are and all that is of God. Remember your oneness and remember me.

# Final Attunement

Imagine the crown of your head opening.
Envision a clear, clean, loving light pouring into your being.

Bring your attention to your throat. Soften your throat.
You have an important message.

Bring your energy to your gut.
This is your power center, your personal connecting place with Spirit.

Bow to the earth.
Be grateful and remember.

You are divine.

Thank you, dear reader,
for joining me on this adventure.

I celebrate your divine, unique Spirit,
and am honored our lives have connected.

I wish you joy.
I wish you miracles.
May you always remember—you are a miracle.

# Acknowledgements

My life has been blessed by many wonderful individuals who have inspired my work. First and foremost, I want to thank my workshop students, readers, and Reiki and Feng Shui clients. You have entrusted me with the role of supporting you in your soul's journey. I am grateful to have had this privilege.

I also thank the many wonderful teachers, role models, mentors and healers who have provided me with encouragement and support on my life's path. These include Kate Appel, Sara Holcombe, Denise Linn, Jane Morris, Suzanne Phillips, Nancy SantoPietro, Nancy Rosanoff, Julie Jordan Scott, Donna Sherman, Stacey Simpson, John Windwalker and Janet Wolf.

I would also like to thank Louise Hay for her wonderful work and in particular, her book *You Can Heal Your Life*, which I discovered in 1993 and was instrumental in the start of my journey in doing this work. I am also grateful to Rosemary Altea, Barbara Brennan, Julia Cameron, Wayne Dyer, Debbie Ford, Rob Jokel, SARK (Susan Ariel Rainbow Kennedy), Elizabeth Lesser, Caroline Myss, John Perkins, Sanaya Roman, Mona Lisa Schultz, Iyanla Vanzant, Doreen Virtue and Marianne Williamson, whose workshops and books offered powerful affirmation on my own journey. I am also grateful to The Omega Institute for Holistic Studies in Rhinebeck, NY for providing wonderful forums through which many of these connections occurred.

Some of the greatest miracles in my life have been my close friendships, many with individuals who have come into my life at the perfect time, and have supported me in moving forward with sharing this work. I thank Jill Cifelli, who is my career angel and also the person who most inspires me with her deep heart and the way she sees humor in her own growth path; Lyenochka Djakov, whom I trusted with this book before I even knew what it was, and is one of my best friends and strongest people I know; and Jacqueline Genovesi, who constantly amazes me with her strength and gifts in working with nature.

I am also deeply grateful to Hilary Purtell, who read the manuscript and provided helpful encouragement and editorial feedback, and to Katie Grant, who helped me brainstorm and move through blocks during a hike down into the Grand Canyon. I also thank the rest of the early group of soul sisters who embarked on the nine-week adventure that resulted from this work, each of whom have acted as midwives, healers and sources of

Acknowledgements

inspiration in their own unique way—June Cook, Katy Kelley, Ileen Nelson, Stacey Simpson and Billie Stewart.

I am grateful to Elizabeth Sullivan for her friendship and sparkle fairies, and her support of my writing; Loren Thorward, for being so real and such a wonderful model of what motherhood is all about; and Dira Strain, Kirsten Brendel, Maria Martin and Klari Nelson, for being such wonderful friends.

I am also infinitely grateful to the many cherished friends I met through my holistic trainings and gatherings including the sacred Soul Coaching, Black Hat Sect Feng Shui, Mandala Yoga, and Wellness Resources communities. Special thanks go to Laurie BonPietro, Renata and Hermod Hansen, Jennifer C. Jackson, Cheryl Smith, Bob Wheeler, Barbara Wingate and Theresa Woodsong, each of who were like angels, coming into my life and supporting me during times of major transformation. I also thank Ruth Beswick, who supported me in this work before I even knew what it was.

I am grateful to the amazing individuals and friends I met through my media relations career including Bob and Pam Chandler, Gianfranco Chicco, Karen DiBernardo, Laurie Flatt, Donna Pepe, Cynthia Rohde, Alice Tischio, Leslie Todtfeld, Susan Tomsky, and a special thank you to Ron Brandsdorfer for his steadfast friendship, encouragement, opportunities, and editorial expertise.

I am blessed to have a strong family offering the immense love, acceptance and humor that have been and will always be my source of connectedness and rootedness in this world. I thank my mother Barbara Jean Sanford Smith for her love, acceptance and support of me exactly as I have been in each moment, her immense compassion and friendship and for telling me as a child that she *knew* I would write a book that would be published someday, and for saying it with such conviction that I believed her. I thank my father Hugh Smith III, for being my inspiration as a writer, for staying up with me into the wee hours of the morning helping me to edit papers so they were 'just right,' for telling me stories as a child, and for always encouraging me to go for my dreams. Both my parents are examples as to how I would like to live, in particular in their unwavering commitment and love for Spirit and each other.

I am also very grateful to my grandmother Olga Kaciuryna Smith Joiner, who gave me my first visualization tape when I was a teenager, and has inspired me with the mental power she possesses, as well as her deep spiritual faith and positive attitude.

I thank my brother Hugh Smith for his laughter, play and integrity; his wife Ann for her friendship and sisterhood; my sister Kim Smith for being such an incredible friend and giving, sensitive soul; her husband Jan Debyser for his play, adventurous spirit and ever-constant offer of help to our family; my brother Scott Smith for always being there for me and making me laugh; and his wife Sharon for her strength and friendship.

I am incredibly blessed to have in-laws I love and respect, and thank them for their loyalty, laughter, acceptance, generous spirits, and sense of family. I thank

## Acknowledgements

my mother- and father-in-law Mary and Jim Bowbliss and my sisters and brothers Trish and Tom Thompson, Bunny and Larry Wisnewski, Christine and Edward Herman and John Bowbliss.

I celebrate my nieces and nephews Alina and Katia Smith Debyser, Kelly and Edward Herman, Michael Karlen, Krystan and Johnny Offerman, Hannah and Aidan Smith, Jacinda Wesolowski and Allison Wisnewski for continually making me smile and reminding me what life is really about. I am also grateful to my extended family members for their support, especially to Kit Hartman, for providing a first home to an early manuscript.

Most of all, I thank my own dear, sweet family. I thank my son Devin James for teaching me what love, compassion and happiness really are, and for filling my world with wonder and delight. I am deeply honored and privileged to be his mother.

And I thank my husband Jim for being my best friend, soul mate, partner, fellow adventurer and the most incredibly grounded, compassionate, patient, playful and fun person I know. I also thank him for his technical assistance, and ongoing support of my work and this book.

# Ready to embark on another adventure?

**The sequel to this book:**
*Spirit In Disguise: A Guide to Miraculous Living, Book 2*
**is now available.**

Meet the spirit guides and Wise Friends who join author Laurie Smith as her meditative adventure continues. In each chapter of this special book, you will meet a different teacher, each with a valuable lesson on how to let go of the past and manifest miracles.

This powerful, delightful book taps the childlike guru within who has always known all things are possible. *Spirit In Disguise* can help you transform your life in magical ways.

---

To order your copy, visit:

**www.lauriesmith.com**

or send your request to:

**Spreading Sunshine Books**
**P.O. Box 692**
**Tiburon, CA 94920**

Printed in the United States
98819LV00002B/47/A